POINT TO POINT BACKEND TESTING IN SOFTWARE DEVELOPMENT

PRIYESH KUMAR PANDEY

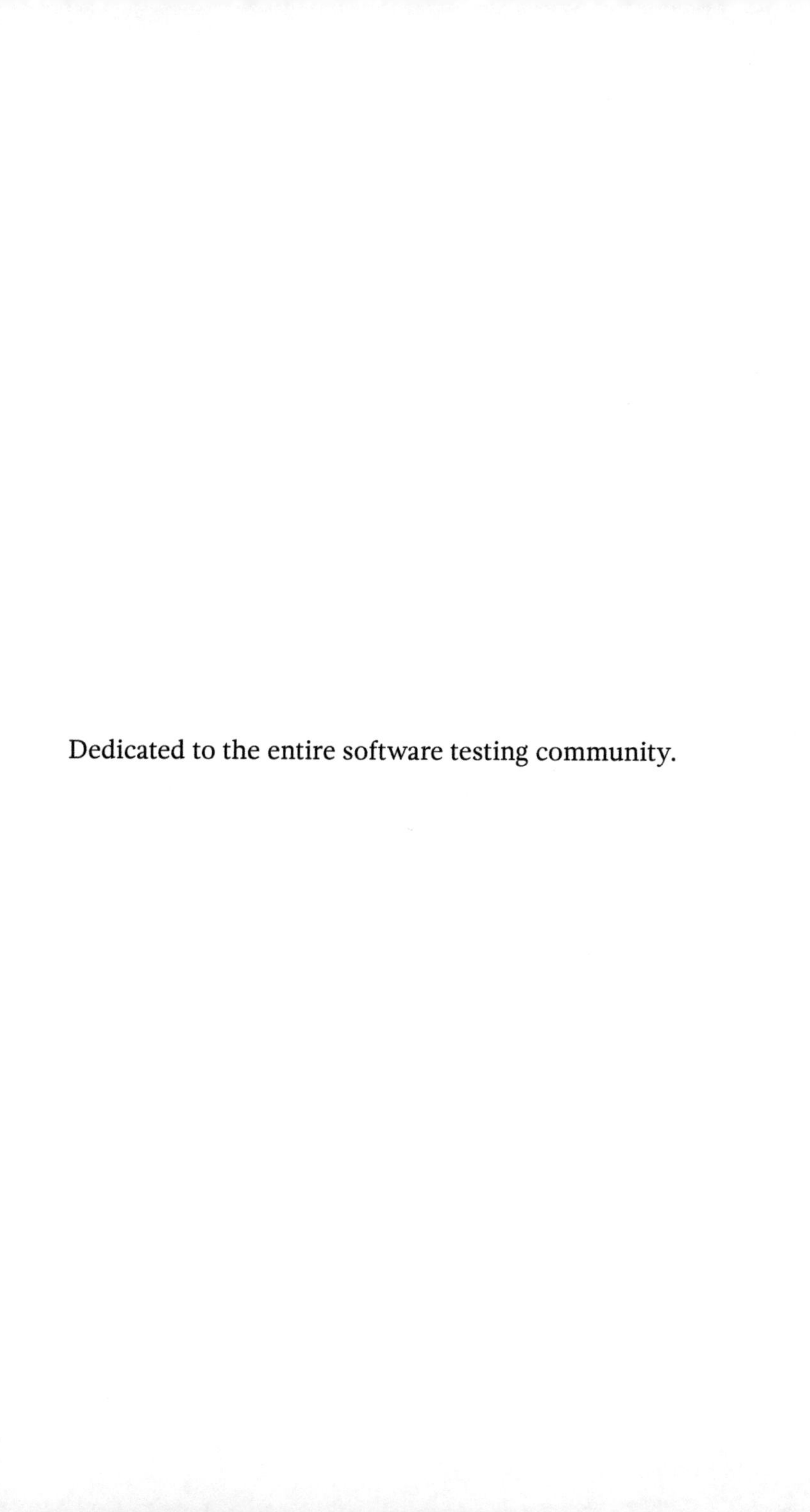

Dedicated to the entire software testing community.

Contents

Preface

This book is intended to provide a very concise overview of the backend testing involved in software development.

This can help a person new to the field of backend testing to provide an introduction and also provide pointers towards planning the career growth in backend testing and in general in the field of software testing. This can also be useful for people not fully aware of the nuances in the backend testing for a better appreciation of the work involved. And as everyone's time is precious, this book is kept short so it can be completed within one sitting.

Keeping in the spirit of this book of being point to point, let's get started.

List Of Abbreviations

API: Application Programming Interface

CI/CD: Continuous Integration / Continuous Development

CIA: Confidentiality, Integrity and Availability - Triad of the Security Principles

CRUD: Create, Retrieve, Update and Delete - Basic operations for database manipulation

ELK: Stack for capturing logs and their visualization implemented by using Elasticsearch, Logstash and Kibana

ETL: Process of Extract, Transform and Load in databases

HTTP: Hyper-Text Transfer Protocol

JDBC: Java Database Connectivity

NoSQL: Database systems which are not implemented as per Relational Model of Relational Databases

PoC: Proof of Concept

RDBMS: Relational Database Management System

REST: Representational State Transfer

SQL: Sequential Query Language

UI: User Interface

URL: Unique Resource Locator

CHAPTER I

Birds-Eye Architecture for Typical Backend

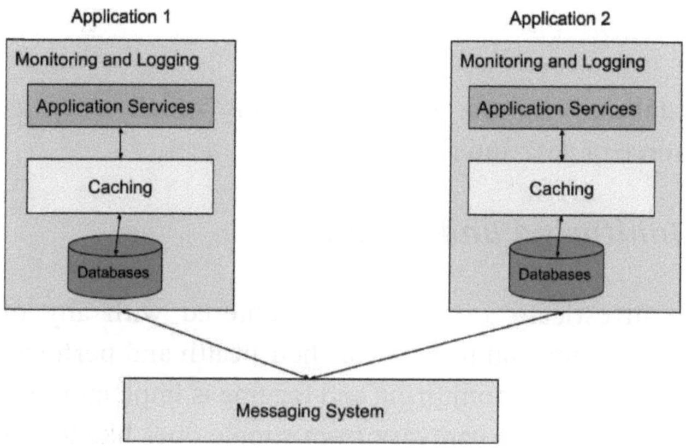

Abstract Architechture of Typical Application Stack

Explanation of the Architecture

Application Services

These are the services or the microservices that have the API endpoints. The API endpoints usually represent an unit of business functionality

Caching

Caching is usually implemented to increase the performance of data retrieval. It is implemented usually to be placed between the services and the RDBMS data sources.

Databases

Databases are the RDBMS systems which work as the source of data and their schemas.

Monitoring and Logging

To investigate any issues encountered with any of the components and to monitor their health and performance, some form of monitoring and logging is implemented. This implementation can vary from simple ones like log files to advanced ones like using ELK stack.

Messaging System

When different applications or services have to communicate with each other, the best practice is to use a messaging system. The messaging system facilitates a standard and high performance for the traffic between various applications.

CHAPTER II

Scope of Backend Testing

Application Services

Validation of the contract

Validation is done whether the APIs are using the right format for the requests, responses, headers and params

Schema Validation

Validation is done to check the structure of requests and responses with their data types

Integration Validation

Validation is done to check the data flow across upstream to downstream applications or systems. Sometimes this may be referred as end-to-end validation for a particular service

Databases

Transactional Validation

This refers to dynamic and ongoing data changes in the databases caused by running any type of functional flows by any means like APIs or UI. This type of validation involves generation of such transactions and then validating data updates in databases

Source of Truth for API data

Many test strategies consider the database as the source of truth for validating the data returned by APIs of a service

ETL Validations

In case of ETL, the validations include ensuring that data integrity is maintained across the transformed schemas. Few examples of scenarios for doing ETL validation are database migration, database redesign, warehousing or archiving of data.

Messaging Infrastructure

Message Format Validation

The format of messages being sent to the messaging systems is checked

Source to Destination Flow

The messages are validated being sent to the messaging system and then picked up by the destination system and processed properly

Security

As multiple applications can send and pick messages from the same messaging system, it is important to ensure that these messages are secured and only be written and read by authorized applications

Scalability

If the messaging system is not a high performing and high availability system, it can easily become a bottleneck. Hence, scalability tests are important here

Caching Infrastructure

Schema Validation

The structure and data types of the objects being stored in the caching system need to be ensured as designed.

Data Integrity

It needs to be ensured that stale data is not being read from the cache and data integrity is reliable

Security

Many applications can deal with sensitive data which are cached, hence it needs to be ensured that it is secure in the caching systems

Scalability

Caching is used for increasing the performance of data retrieval, hence they should not be creating bottlenecks. Hence testing for scalability is important

Logging and Monitoring Infrastructure

Debugging and Investigation

In most scenarios it is used for investigating any issues by either analyzing the logs and metrics manually or automating the alerts for specific conditions

Funnel Analysis

In many scenarios logging and monitoring enables analysis of flow of traffic across the system.

CHAPTER III

Process of Backend Testing

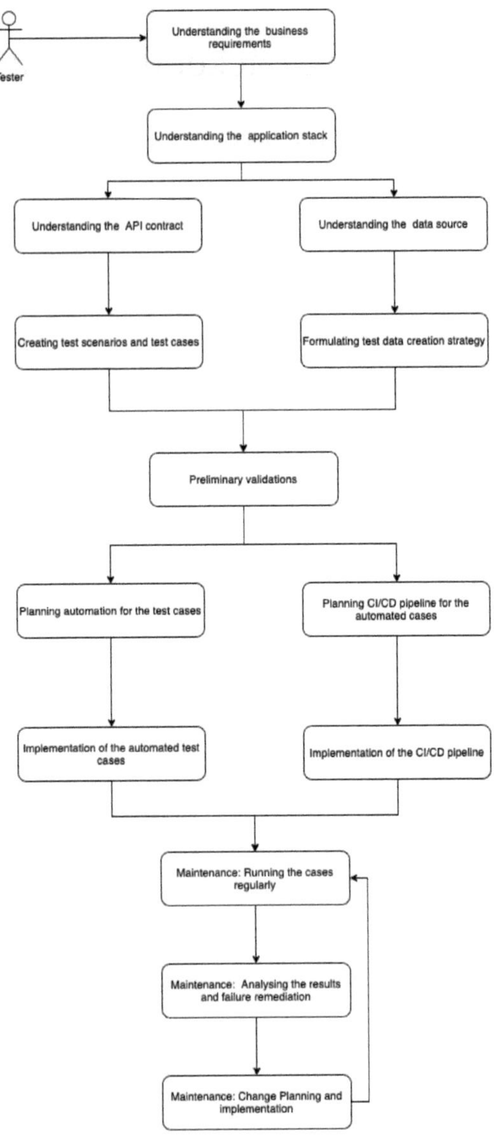

Flow chart for the process of backend testing

Understanding the business requirements

- Understanding the data flow across components
- Understanding the business impact and value

Understanding the application stack

- Understanding the technologies used for implementation
- Understanding the reason behind the choice of the technologies for each stack i.e. service, database, caching, logging and monitoring
- Understanding how these are configured and deployed
- Understanding the deployment infrastructure

Understanding the API contract

- Understanding the request and response structures
- Gaining knowledge of endpoints, their parameters, custom headers and typical requests and responses
- Understanding all possible methods and response code scenarios for each endpoint

Understanding the data source

- Understanding the schemas in the data source used for a service
- Understanding the sources of each endpoints for the data
- Understanding the mappings between the data source and the API contract i.e. parameters, headers, requests and responses

Creating test scenarios and test cases

- Usually creating scenarios and test cases for backend testing the black box testing techniques are used, as we really don't need to understand the actual code
- Most relevant techniques for API test scenarios and test cases are equivalence class partitioning, boundary value analysis

Formulating test data creation strategy

- Running tests requires generation of test data to simulate all the tests
- An appropriate test strategy is developed based on the understanding of technology stack and the developed test cases
- Typical generation techniques can be direct insertions or updates in the data source, using the existing APIs to generate data, using any upstream systems to generate the data, loading test data as part of the deployment, loading sanitized data from other environments

Preliminary validations

- Preliminary validations include using any of the tools for calling the API and visually validating the contracts
- Typical tools for API validations are Postman and curl
- For database validation the corresponding database client is used

Planning automation for the test cases

- Preliminary validations can help in understanding the typical usage of APIs, databases, caching, logging and monitoring systems
- This understanding can be used to plan the automation of most used and impactful tasks
- Automation is planned typically like application development and at highest level may have stages like defining requirements, coding and dry running the tests
- During the planning phase a choice of the tools and technologies is made. This choice can be based on PoCs done during this phase

Planning CI/CD pipeline for the automated cases

- Parallely with automating the tests, CI/CD pipeline implementation is also planned

- It is important to have CI/CD pipeline built which as the automated tests as its part to realize the value of automated cases
- CI/CD planning can include choice of the tools based on the technology stack and infrastructure, defining stages of the pipeline and deployment of the pipeline
- Typical tools used for are Jenkins, Hudson, GitLab's jobs, GitHub's Actions, Chef and many others (use Google to search popular tools)
- To choose a tool, evaluation can be done by doing PoCs with candidate tools

Implementation of the automated test cases

- Implementation phase of automated tests involves with the designing, coding and dry runs of the tests
- This implementation can be from scratch or using an existing framework
- To maintain the quality of automated tests a regular review of code and runs of the tests is one of the best practices

Implementation of the CI/CD pipeline

- Implementation phase of CI/CD pipeline involves using the automated tests as part of the continuous integration and development i.e. running the tests whenever anything changes in the system

- A change can be in code, the way of deployment, changes in data source schemas, changes in the infrastructure or changes in the tests
- Implementation is done using the existing tools used in the team or organization or using the choice of the tool made during evaluation and PoCs

Maintenance: Running the cases regularly

- It is important to run the test cases regularly to realize their value and make changes so that the tests are not obsolete
- Best practice for this is to run it as part of scheduled CI/CD pipelines

Maintenance: Analyzing the results and failure remediation

- To understand the health of application and the test cases, a regular analysis of the automated test results is required
- To enable efficient analysis many tasks can be automated like building a dashboard of the results, applying automated analysis and categorizing typical failures
- Some level of manual analysis is expected to get a holistic view of the application and test's health
- The analysis may result in an action for remediation like fixing the application or fixing the automated tests

Maintenance: Change planning and implementation

- Based on the analysis of the test results a change needs to be planned either in the application, infrastructure or the test
- This will start another iteration of development of either the application or the tests

CHAPTER IV

Tools for Validation of APIs

Here is a typical list of tools used for validation of services or APIs. This indicates the more popular ones and is not an exhaustive list.

Curl: For basic understanding of Curl and its commands, refer to this page.

Postman: Refer Postman's page https://www.postman.com/

RestAssured: Java library for API automation and more suitable for functional testing. More expressive for business users. More information on their homepage https://rest-assured.io/

Apache HTTP: Java library for low level API calls. More useful if fine grained control is required for API calls. More information on their homepage https://hc.apache.org/httpcomponents-client-5.1.x/

OkHttp: This is a high performing Java and Android library for implementing HTTP calls. It supports HTTP/2 as well. More information on their homepage https://square.github.io/okhttp/

WebClient: This is part of Spring Framework and is a non-blocking, reactive client to perform HTTP requests. Refer its documentation here

RestTemplate: It is a synchronous client and also part of Spring Framework. Refer its documentation here

CHAPTER V

Tools for Database Validation

SQL client: The database clients for the respective RDBMS products, like SQL Workbench, Oracle SQL Developer, MSSQL, SQLPro for Postgres and many others can be used for visual validations and understanding of schemas

Database drivers for automated validations: For executing queries from code, corresponding database drivers are used for the respective programming languages like JDBC for Java

CRUD Repositories: There are frameworks which provide features for executing database queries. And these may support not only RDBMS products but also NoSQL products. An example is the repositories in Spring framework

CHAPTER VI

Important Aspects of API Testing

Request/Response validations: This is the most heavily done validations. This validation typically involves serialization/deserialization of requests and responses and validating their structure and the data

Validation of all possible response types: An endpoint can return multiple status codes based on the data passed to it. Covering all possible status codes returned increases the test coverage, hence it is important to implement it

Functional flow validation: Simulating a typical user behavior by using API endpoints is way to test integrations across upstream and downstream applications

Scalability validations: The APIs and to be more accurate the funnel (the data flow across various components) that gets huge traffic needs to scale well and for this scalability tests can be performed using any of the performance testing tools like Jmeter, Gatling, Locust and many more

Security validations: The API for secure applications require validations for security aspects to ensure adherence to CIA (Confidentiality, Integrity, Availability) principles

CHAPTER VII

Practice for Backend Testing

There are a lot of static mock APIs present over the Internet to do very basic "Hello World" types of practice with API automation. Below is a description of a mock service that can be easily deployed on a personal computer and can be used for practicing API validations either visually by tools like curl or Postman or by writing code for automated tests.

Prerequisites

Docker Installation - Install Docker Desktop from here

Getting Started

- Run command docker pull priyeshkpandeysf/mock-service:latest to pull the image
- To start the container execute command: docker run -p 11000:11000 --name mock-service priyeshkpandeysf/mock-service
- Note the following values from the startup logs, which will be used later

```
INFO H2ConsoleAutoConfiguration - H2 console available at '/h2-console'. Database available at 'jdbc:h2:file:/Users/priyeshpandey/playground/mock-data'
```

```
Using generated security password: 5a715c20-2f67-476a-aa33-0182f8930e41
```

Logs line to note database url and login password for UI

Features

- Implementation of a RESTful service to mimic the usual use cases taking an e-commerce domain terminologies
- Flexibility to generate own data by accessing the DB from console
- An endpoint that has redirection, to practice with such scenarios (like payments)
- Swagger UI to try out the APIs manually without the need of tools like Postman or curl
- Also enables learning by exploring the APIs and their intended functionality

Accessing the Database Console

- After starting the service, visit http://localhost:11000/h2-console in your browser
- This will open the database console as shown below

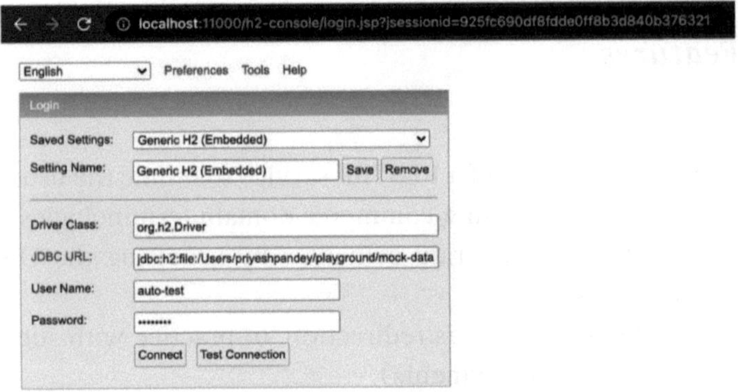

Opening the database console in the browser

- Replace the JDBC URL as captured from the logs (shown in the screenshot in the Getting Started section)
- Provide auto-test as the user name
- Provide password as P@ssW0rD
- Click Connect. This will display the tables and the console where you can execute SQL queries
- You can use this console to create your own data for your practice

Database console after logging in

Accessing Swagger UI

- Open Swagger UI by opening the url http://localhost:11000/swagger-ui/index.html in your browser
- This will display the Swagger UI like shown below
- You can use this to execute the APIs from the Swagger UI to explore the APIs

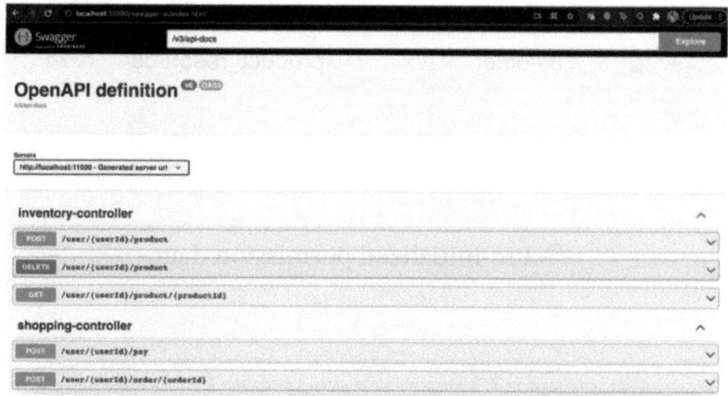

Swagger UI for the mock service endpoints

Pre-Initialized Data

- Following data is pre-initialized and some logic in the APIs depend on them

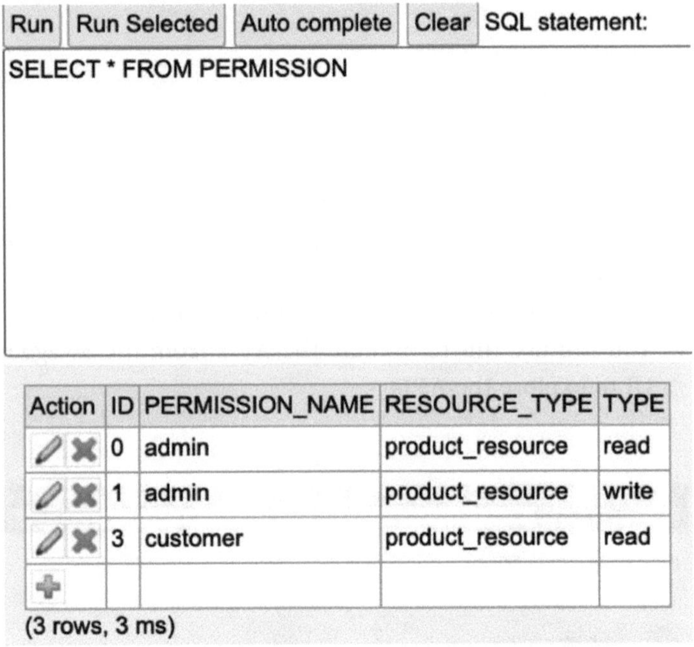

Run | Run Selected | Auto complete | Clear | SQL statement:

```
SELECT * FROM PERMISSION
```

Action	ID	PERMISSION_NAME	RESOURCE_TYPE	TYPE
	0	admin	product_resource	read
	1	admin	product_resource	write
	3	customer	product_resource	read

(3 rows, 3 ms)

Pre-initialized permission data

Run | Run Selected | Auto complete | Clear | SQL statement:

SELECT * FROM ROLE

Action	ID	PERMISSION_NAME	ROLE_NAME
	0	admin	admin
	1	customer	customer

(2 rows, 2 ms)

Pre-initialized role data

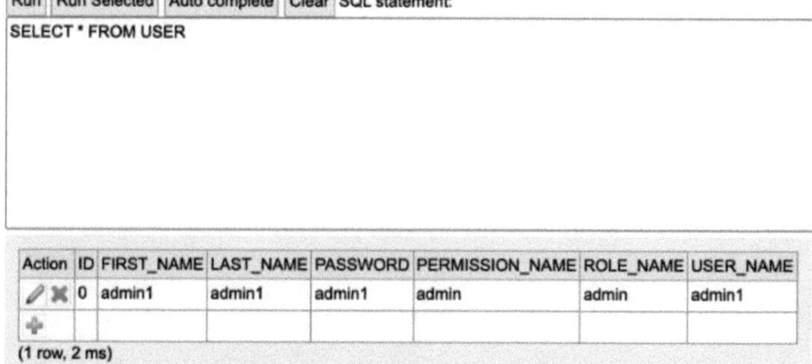

Run | Run Selected | Auto complete | Clear | SQL statement:

SELECT * FROM USER

Action	ID	FIRST_NAME	LAST_NAME	PASSWORD	PERMISSION_NAME	ROLE_NAME	USER_NAME
	0	admin1	admin1	admin1	admin	admin	admin1

(1 row, 2 ms)

Pre-initialized user data

Functionality Notes

- The POST /signup endpoint creates users only with customer role and permissions

Contact for Issue Resolution

- Drop an email to info@knowyoursf.com for any issues

CHAPTER VIII

Skill Matrix for Backend Testing

Below is a skills requirement matrix that I have seen at most of the place in my experience. The first column represents the required skill and the next three columns represent the level of expertise. The first occurrence of the tick in the expertise level columns represent the minimum level of expertise for the skill in that row.

Skill / Expertise Level	Beginner	Intermediate	Expert
Programming		✓	✓
Problem Solving		✓	✓
Application Tech Stack		✓	✓
Deployment Infrastructure	✓	✓	✓
Serialization/Deserialization		✓	✓
HTTP	✓	✓	✓
RDBMS		✓	✓
NoSQL		✓	✓
Maven		✓	✓
Git		✓	✓
TestNg		✓	✓
Cucumber		✓	✓

Skill requirements matrix for backend testing

CHAPTER IX

Requirements for a Good Backend Automation Framework

When we are developing a Backend Automation Framework, the following are the typical requirements for it to cater to the requirements as the application and the tests both evolve over time.

- Separation of Business and Technical aspects
- Loose coupling between framework code and automation library
- Adherence to SOLID design principles
- Easy discoverability for test developers
- Easy to change code
- Easy to deploy in development pipelines
- Easy to run for demo or learning

Summary

In a very short time, an overview and various nuances of the backend testing in software development has been covered. This can enable you to take informed decisions and plan the career roadmap for a software testing professional. Even if you are a non-technical person this can provide an appreciation for the people working in the field of software testing in general and in the field of backend testing specifically.

You can also use this as a quick reference whenever some terms come up in the context of backend testing in software development.

9 798888 058008

Printed by Libri Plureos GmbH in Hamburg, Germany